The GREEN BOOK of Must Know Stories

To
Edward.
7.6.2009
First Holy Communion

Written and illustrated by Alexander Brown

luv
Gargan

© Alexander Brown 2008
First published 2008
ISBN 978 1 84427 324 9

Scripture Union, 207–209 Queensway, Bletchley, Milton
Keynes, MK2 2EB, UK
Email: info@scriptureunion.org.uk
Website: www.scriptureunion.org.uk

Scripture Union Australia, Locked Bag 2, Central Coast
Business Centre, NSW 2252, Australia
Website: www.scriptureunion.org.au

Scripture Union USA, PO Box 987, Valley Forge, PA 19482,
USA
Website: www.scriptureunion.org

British Library Cataloguing-in-Data.
A catalogue record of this book is available from the British
Library.

Printed and bound in China by 1010 Printing International Ltd
Cover design by Paul Airy: four-nine-zero design

Scripture Union is an international charity working with
churches in more than 130 countries, providing resources to
bring the good news of Jesus Christ to children, young people
and families and to encourage them to develop spiritually
through the Bible and prayer.

As well as our network of volunteers, staff and associates who
run holidays, church-based events and school Christian groups,
we produce a wide range of publications and support those who
use our resources through training programmes.

Noah and the ark

This story takes place a very, very long time ago.

It is the story of a man called Noah and how he and his family and all the animals of the world were kept safe by God.

It seemed that almost everyone on the whole earth was doing very bad things.

This made God really sad. He was sorry he had created the world. But God had a plan.

The only man on the planet to behave in a way that pleased God was Noah. God shared his plan with Noah. He gave him very clear instructions.

There was going to be a huge flood. Noah had to build an enormous boat called an ark. It had to have many rooms.

God would bring to Noah two of every kind of animal so that the world could carry on after the flood.

It took Noah a long time but at last the ark was finished. God told Noah to take his family into the ark – three sons, their wives and his own wife. God told Noah to take all the animals into the ark too. Once they were safely inside, God shut the door.

The terrible flood began.

Water underneath the earth burst through the ground. Water above the earth rained down like never before. This went on and on for forty days and forty nights.

Even the highest mountains were under the water. After the flood had finished, Noah's ark got stuck on the top of a mountain. As the water went down, his family could see the mountains again.

Noah sent out a dove to see if it could find anything growing. The first time it just flew about, with nowhere to land. A week later, Noah did this again. The dove came back with a twig in its beak. A week later the dove didn't even come back. Noah knew it was safe to leave the ark.

God promised Noah that he would never flood the earth again. He showed Noah a rainbow in the sky as a sign of his promise.

God's ten rules

Moses was one of the greatest men in the Bible. God used Moses and his big brother, Aaron, to lead God's people. They were camping at the bottom of the Sinai Mountain, getting close to their new land. It was here that God gave Moses the top ten rules for living. This is what happened.

Years ago, God had first spoken to Moses through a burning bush.

Now Moses and all God's people knew God was going to speak to them. They waited and waited for three days.

On the third day...

...thunder and lightning filled the air.
The noise of trumpets blasted everywhere.
A cloud covered the top of the mountain.
The whole mountain trembled.

Moses asked God's people to stand at the foot of
the mountain. God ordered Moses to come up the
mountain. Everyone else was to stay where they
were.

At the top, God gave Moses two big pieces of stone.
On them God had written his ten rules for life.
These ten rules would make sure that the people
lived together peacefully, and served God
in a way that pleased him.

Today, people call these
'The Ten Commandments'.

Here are the ten rules:

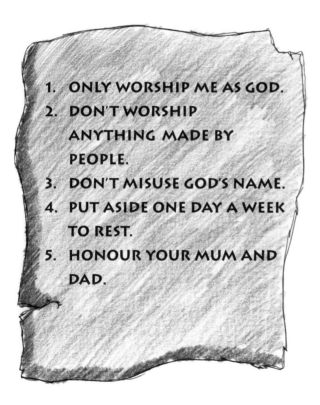

1. ONLY WORSHIP ME AS GOD.
2. DON'T WORSHIP ANYTHING MADE BY PEOPLE.
3. DON'T MISUSE GOD'S NAME.
4. PUT ASIDE ONE DAY A WEEK TO REST.
5. HONOUR YOUR MUM AND DAD.

6. DON'T MURDER.
7. STAY FAITHFUL IN MARRIAGE.
8. DON'T STEAL.
9. DON'T LIE.
10. DON'T BE JEALOUS OF OTHER PEOPLE'S THINGS.

They were so important that God's people made a special box to carry these stones in. They carried them everywhere they travelled.

stone tablets in here

They needed to learn these ten rules by heart and obey them.

Jesus feeds over 5000!

Everywhere Jesus went, crowds of people turned up to listen to him. So one day, Jesus took his friends to a place in the hills where they would be able to get some peace and quiet. But people soon discovered where Jesus had gone. Before too long, Jesus and his friends were once again surrounded by people.

Jesus

Jesus' friends listening

Jesus welcomed everyone. He was a fabulous storyteller and teacher. He spoke to them about God's kingdom. He healed people who were sick. It was amazing!

He kept going until it began to get dark. Jesus' friends began to get worried!

His friends looked around. They were in the middle of nowhere, and only had enough food for themselves! What would happen to all these people?

They gave Jesus some advice. "We need to send these people away, or they'll have nothing to eat."

But Jesus said, "You feed them!"

The disciples were confused.

"We only have five bread rolls and two small fish," they said. "How is that going to feed this huge crowd? There are over 5,000 men here. And thousands more women and children."

very confused

very small lunch

Jesus smiled.

He told his friends to make the crowd sit down in groups of about fifty people.

He took the five bread rolls and two fish.

He thanked God for the food, and broke it all up.

He told the disciples to share it out with everyone.

The disciples did what they were told.
They found that there was enough for everyone.
In fact, there was more than enough!
There were twelve baskets full of leftover broken pieces.

They should have known.
After all, when Jesus was around, anything could happen.

The good Samaritan

Jesus told this story to help people think about who they should care about.

Once upon a time there lived a man who travelled a lot because of his work.

One day, while he was walking along a lonely road, he was attacked by some robbers! Before he knew what had happened, he was left with no money, torn clothes, and lots of cuts.

He thought he was going to die.

As he lay there, a man came by.

Everyone knew this man was very, very good. Surely the very, very good man would stop to help.

But instead, he crossed the road to the other side and just carried on walking.

Next, a man came past who belonged to a club called "We're kind to others". Surely this kind man would stop to help.

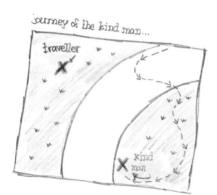

But instead, he crossed the road to the other side and just carried on walking.

Much later, a man came by who was a Samaritan.

Samaritans were foreigners. No one trusted them. Surely the Samaritan would not stop to help!

But when the Samaritan saw the traveller, he stopped to help him. He put plasters and bandages on his cuts.

He took him to a guest house where he could be looked after.

To the surprise of everyone, a few days later the Samaritan came back again. He paid the owner of the guest house to go on caring for the traveller. Amazing!

The big question is this: in this story who was the traveller's friend? Which man was really good and kind?

new best friends

Jesus told his listeners to be like the Samaritan.

The runaway son

This is a story that Jesus told about a boy who ran away, his angry older brother, and a father who loved them both.

Once upon a time there was a rich farmer who had two sons. One day, the younger son asked his dad this question.

"Dad, when you die I'm going to have half of all you own, right?"

"Yes, son," said the father.

"I want my half now. I'm leaving home."

The father was deeply hurt, but he gave his son half of all he owned.

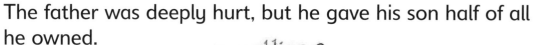

The son promptly left home.
He began to spend his new-found wealth.

One day he ran out of money. He would have to get himself a job. But the only job he could find was working on a farm, feeding and cleaning out the pigs.

his dream meal

???

PIGS   PIGS

not having fun

PIGWORLD.COM

FUN! FUN! FUN!

pigs

A huge famine swept across the land. No one had any food. No one gave the son anything. He got so hungry that the pig food looked good to eat!

all is forgiven

Suddenly he came to his senses.

"What have I been thinking!" he said. "Servants in Dad's house always have food. I'll go home and say, 'Father, I've done wrong. Please forgive me and accept me back as a servant.'"

He packed up and went home. But while he still had a long way to go, his dad saw him. His dad ran to meet him. His dad was so thrilled to see him.

"Dad, I've done wrong..." the son began.

But the father hugged him. "I forgive you," he whispered. He then said to his servants, "Quick, we're going to have a party. Get the best clothes out for my son. Put the family ring on his finger. This son was lost, but now he's found!"

The older brother heard the noise of the party.
"It's not fair!" he grumbled. "My lazy brother comes home, and you treat him as special!"

"Everything I own is yours," the father said. "But we have to have a party now. Your brother has come back. He was lost, but now he's found."